INTRODUCTION

The ability to sight-read fluently is a most important part of your instrumental training. Yet the *study* of sight-reading is often badly neglected by young players and is frequently regarded as no more than a rather unpleasant side-line. If you become a *good* sight-reader you will be able to learn pieces more quickly, and play in ensembles with confidence and assurance. Also, in grade examinations, good performance in the sight-reading test will result in useful extra marks!

Using the workbook

The purpose of this workbook is to incorporate sight-reading regularly into your practice and lessons, and to help you prepare for the sight-reading test in grade examinations. It offers you a progressive series of enjoyable and stimulating stages in which, with careful work, you should show considerable improvement from week to week.

Each stage consists of two parts: firstly, exercises which you should prepare in advance, along with a short piece with questions; and secondly, an unprepared test, to be found at the end of the book.

Your teacher will mark your work according to accuracy. Each stage carries a maximum of 50 marks and your work will be assessed as follows:

> 2 marks for each of the six questions relating to the prepared piece (total 12).
> 18 marks for the prepared piece itself.
> 20 marks for the unprepared test. (Teachers should devise a similar series of questions for the unprepared test, and take the answers into account when allocating a final mark.)

Space is given at the end of each stage for you to keep a running total of your marks as you progress. If you are scoring 40 or more each time you are doing well!

At the top of the first page in each stage you will see one or two new features to be introduced. There are then normally four different types of exercise:

1 **Rhythmic exercises** It is very important that you should be able to feel and maintain a steady beat. These exercises will help develop this ability. There are at least four ways of doing them: clap or tap the lower line (the beat) while singing the upper line to 'la'; tap the lower line with your foot and clap the upper line; on a table or flat surface, tap the lower line with one hand and the upper line with the other; 'play' the lower line on a metronome and clap or tap the upper line.

2 **Melodic exercises** Fluent sight-reading depends on recognising melodic shapes at first glance. These shapes are often related to scales and arpeggios. Before you begin, always notice the *key-signature* and the notes affected by it, along with any accidentals.

3 **A prepared piece with questions** You should prepare carefully both the piece and the questions, which are to help you think about and understand the piece before you play it. Put your answers in the spaces provided.

4 **An unprepared piece** Finally, your teacher will give you an *unprepared* test to be read at *sight*.

Remember to count throughout each piece and to keep going at a steady and even tempo. Always try to look ahead, at least to the next note or beat.

STAGE 1

$$\frac{3}{8} + \frac{4}{8}$$

RHYTHMIC EXERCISES

MELODIC EXERCISES

Improve Your Sight-reading!

A workbook for examinations

Saxophone

Grades 4 and 5

Paul Harris

£ 4.50

FABER ff MUSIC

NAME	
EXAMINATION RECORD	

GRADE	DATE	MARK

TEACHER'S NAME	
TELEPHONE	

© 1995 by Faber Music Ltd.
First published in 1995 by Faber Music Ltd.
3 Queen Square, London WC1N 3AU
Cover design by S & M Tucker
Music and text set by Wessex Music Services
Printed in England

The **Improve Your Sight-reading!** series

Piano Pre-Grade 1	ISBN 0 571 51528 2	Oboe Grades 1, 2 & 3	ISBN 0 571 51633 5
Piano Grade 1	ISBN 0 571 51241 0	Oboe Grades 4 & 5	ISBN 0 571 51634 3
Piano Grade 2	ISBN 0 571 51242 9	Saxophone Grades 1, 2 & 3	ISBN 0 571 51635 1
Piano Grade 3	ISBN 0 571 51243 7	Saxophone Grades 4 & 5	ISBN 0 571 51636 X
Piano Grade 4	ISBN 0 571 51244 5		
Piano Grade 5	ISBN 0 571 51245 3	*Grade 1-5 books*	
Piano Grade 6	ISBN 0 571 51330 1	Viola	ISBN 0 571 51075 2
Piano Grade 7	ISBN 0 571 51331 X	Cello	ISBN 0 571 51027 2
Piano Grade 8	ISBN 0 571 51332 8	Double bass	ISBN 0 571 51149 X
Violin Grade 1	ISBN 0 571 51385 9	Bassoon	ISBN 0 571 51148 1
Violin Grade 2	ISBN 0 571 51386 7	Horn	ISBN 0 571 51076 0
Violin Grade 3	ISBN 0 571 51387 5	Trumpet	ISBN 0 571 50989 4
Violin Grade 4	ISBN 0 571 51388 3	Trombone	ISBN 0 571 51077 9
Violin Grade 5	ISBN 0 571 51389 1		
Violin Supplement	ISBN 0 571 51167 8	*Grade 5-8 books*	
Flute Grades 1, 2 & 3	ISBN 0 571 51466 9	Violin	ISBN 0 571 51153 8
Flute Grades 4 & 5	ISBN 0 571 51467 7	Flute	ISBN 0 571 51150 3
Clarinet Grades 1, 2 & 3	ISBN 0 571 51464 2	Clarinet	ISBN 0 571 51151 1
Clarinet Grades 4 & 5	ISBN 0 571 51465 0	Trumpet	ISBN 0 571 51152 X
Descant recorder			
Grades 1, 2 & 3	ISBN 0 571 51373 5		

PREPARED PIECE

1 In which key is this piece written?

2 What does *Allegretto con moto* mean?

3 What will you count?

4 What are the letter names of the notes in bars 3 and 15?

5 What does the articulation marking ♩♪♪♩ indicate?

6 Which of the following words best describe the character and style of this piece?
Lighthearted, Tragic, Cantabile, Joyful

Total:

Handwritten: Not as fast as allegro   Con = with   moto = movement

Mark:

Prepared work total:

Unprepared:

Total:

Running totals:
1

STAGE 2

For accurate sight-reading it is important to know when to count in sub-divisions of the beat. More difficult rhythms are often made easier by counting in sub-divisions.

RHYTHMIC EXERCISES

MELODIC EXERCISES

PREPARED PIECE

1 In which key is the piece written? Play the appropriate scale in its harmonic or melodic form. ☐

2 What note values will you count and why? ☐

3 Where does the music of the first two bars return? ☐

4 How many beats will you count for the G in bar 2? ☐

5 What is the letter name of the second note in bar 6? ☐

6 Clap this rhythm: ☐

Total: ☐

Moderato

Mark: ☐

Prepared work total: ☐

Unprepared: ☐

Total: ☐

Running totals:

1	2

STAGE 3

RHYTHMIC EXERCISES

MELODIC EXERCISES

PREPARED PIECE

1 How many beats are there in each bar? ☐

2 Mark the accidental with a cross. ☐

3 What does **mf** indicate? ☐

4 What does the marking ♩ indicate? ☐

5 What is the meaning of *Moderato, tempo di minuetto?* ☐

6 Clap this rhythm. ☐

Total: ☐

Moderato, tempo di minuetto

Mark: ☐

Prepared work total: ☐

Unprepared: ☐

Total: ☐

Running totals:

1	2	3

STAGE 4

RHYTHMIC EXERCISES

MELODIC EXERCISES

PREPARED PIECE

1 In which note values will you count this piece?

2 What is the meaning of *Allegro ma non troppo*?

3 In which key is the piece written?

4 What does the sign ⨍ indicate?

5 Mark an accidental with a cross.

6 What is the letter name of the last note in bar 4?

Total:

Allegro ma non troppo

Mark:

Prepared work total:

Unprepared:

Total:

Running totals:

1	2	3	4

STAGE 5

RHYTHMIC EXERCISES

MELODIC EXERCISES

PREPARED PIECE

1 Explain the time-signature. How many beats will you count in each bar? ☐

2 In which key is the piece written? ☐

3 Mark with a cross any notes affected by the key-signature. ☐

4 For how many beats should the B (bars 7-8) be held? ☐

5 What is the meaning of *rall. (rallentando)?*

        cresc. (crescendo)?

        dim. (diminuendo)? ☐

6 What does *Andante sostenuto* mean? ☐

Total: ☐

Mark: ☐

Prepared work total: ☐

Unprepared: ☐

Total: ☐

Running totals:

1	2	3	4	5

STAGE 6

A major

RHYTHMIC EXERCISES

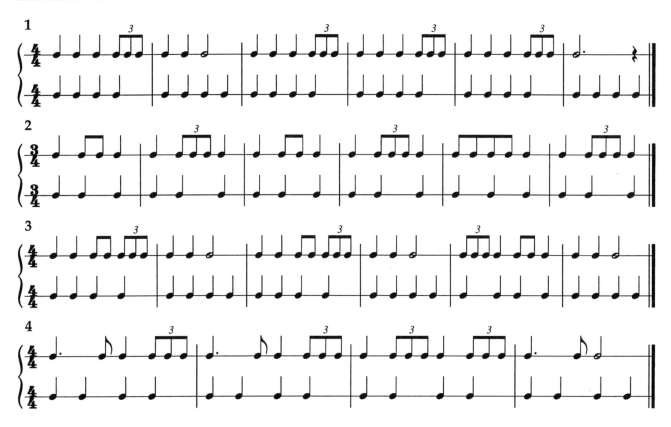

MELODIC EXERCISES

PREPARED PIECE

1 In which key is the piece written? □

2 Mark the G sharps with a cross. □

3 What do the dots under and over the notes indicate? □

4 What does *Allegretto con moto* mean? □

5 What is the character of this piece? □

6 How will you make your performance musical? □

Total: □

Allegretto con moto

Mark: □

Prepared work total: □

Unprepared: □

Total: □

Running totals:

1	2	3	4	5	6

STAGE 7

RHYTHMIC EXERCISES

MELODIC EXERCISES

PREPARED PIECE

1 In which key is this piece written?

2 Which form of the scale is used?

3 How would you describe the character of the music?

4 How will you count this piece?

5 Does the opening idea return - if so, does it differ?

6 What do the dots above and below the notes indicate?

Total:

Allegretto con moto

Mark:

Prepared work total:

Unprepared:

Total:

Running totals:

1	2	3	4	5	6	7

UNPREPARED TESTS
STAGE 1

STAGE 2

3 Con moto

STAGE 4

1 Con fuoco

2 Allegro ma non troppo

3 Allegro

STAGE 5

1 Andante

2 Andante con moto

3 **Con moto**

STAGE 6

1 **Andante**

2 **Allegro animato**

3 **Andantino**

Improve Your Sight-reading!

'Oh no! Not the sight-reading test!'

*The very thought of sight-reading, especially
in examinations, makes most young players groan.
But now more than ever, the ability to sight-read fluently
is an essential part of the training of
musicians on any instrument.*

*This workbook is designed to help overcome sight-reading
problems, especially for saxophonists working for
the grade 4 and 5 examinations.*

*Step by step it helps the player to build up a complete
picture of each piece, first through rhythmic and melodic
exercises related to specific problems,
then by the study of a prepared piece with associated
questions for the student to answer, and so finally
to the real, unprepared sight-reading test itself.
Mark boxes for each stage allow both teacher and pupil
to keep a check of progress.*

It's really not so difficult after all!

ISBN 0-571-51636-X

FABER MUSIC 3 QUEEN SQUARE LONDON